50 Premium Japanese Dinners

By: Kelly Johnson

Table of Contents

- Wagyu Steak
- Sukiyaki (Japanese Hot Pot with Beef)
- Shabu-Shabu (Japanese Fondue with Wagyu)
- Yakiniku (Japanese BBQ)
- Unagi Kabayaki (Grilled Eel with Sweet Soy Glaze)
- Kaiseki Ryori (Traditional Multi-Course Meal)
- Fugu Sashimi (Blowfish Sashimi)
- Matsutake Dobin Mushi (Matsutake Mushroom Soup)
- Kani Nabe (Crab Hot Pot)
- Otoro Sashimi (Fatty Tuna Sashimi)
- Chirashi Sushi with Premium Seafood
- Uni Don (Sea Urchin Rice Bowl)
- Ikura Don (Salmon Roe Rice Bowl)
- Kaisen Don (Mixed Sashimi Rice Bowl)
- Hida Beef Teppanyaki
- Kamameshi (Iron Pot Rice with Seafood or Meat)
- Black Cod Saikyo Yaki (Miso-Marinated Black Cod)
- Nodoguro Shioyaki (Grilled Blackthroat Seaperch)
- Anago Meshi (Grilled Sea Eel Over Rice)
- Amaebi Sashimi (Sweet Shrimp Sashimi)
- Ise Ebi (Spiny Lobster Sashimi or Grilled)
- Kurobuta Tonkatsu (Premium Black Pork Cutlet)
- Soba with Duck Breast
- Dobin Mushi (Tea Pot Steamed Soup)
- Miso-Marinated Wagyu
- Nabe with Kobe Beef
- Abalone Steak with Butter Sauce
- Hokkaido Scallop Sashimi
- Ankimo (Monkfish Liver)
- Crab Miso Soup with Fresh Snow Crab
- Yakitori Omakase (Grilled Skewers with Premium Ingredients)
- Toro Taku Roll (Fatty Tuna & Pickled Radish Roll)
- Sazae Tsuboyaki (Grilled Turban Shell)
- Ishikari Nabe (Salmon Hot Pot)
- Karei Karaage (Deep-Fried Flounder)

- Botan Ebi Sashimi (Large Sweet Shrimp)
- Shojin Ryori (Buddhist Vegan Cuisine)
- Tosa Zukuri (Seared Bonito Sashimi)
- Tai Chazuke (Sea Bream Over Rice with Tea)
- Kinmedai Nitsuke (Simmered Golden Eye Snapper)
- Hamo Ryori (Pike Conger Eel Dishes)
- Tataki Style Wagyu Beef
- Kinki Nitsuke (Simmered Channel Rockfish)
- Premium Hokkaido Uni Pasta
- Miso Black Cod with Truffle Oil
- Foie Gras Chawanmushi (Steamed Egg Custard with Foie Gras)
- Grilled King Crab Legs
- White Truffle Soba
- A5 Wagyu Sukiyaki with Truffle Egg Dip
- Lobster Miso Ramen

Wagyu Steak

Ingredients:

- 1 Wagyu steak (ribeye or sirloin)
- Salt and pepper to taste
- 1 tbsp butter
- 1 clove garlic (crushed)

Instructions:

1. Let the steak rest at room temperature for 30 minutes.
2. Heat a pan over medium-high heat, sear the steak for 2-3 minutes per side.
3. Add butter and garlic, basting the steak until cooked to desired doneness.
4. Rest for 5 minutes before slicing.

Sukiyaki (Japanese Hot Pot with Beef)

Ingredients:

- ½ lb thinly sliced Wagyu beef
- 2 cups dashi
- 2 tbsp soy sauce
- 1 tbsp mirin
- 1 tbsp sugar
- ½ block tofu (cubed)
- 1 cup Napa cabbage (chopped)
- ½ cup mushrooms
- 1 raw egg (for dipping)

Instructions:

1. Heat dashi, soy sauce, mirin, and sugar in a pot.
2. Add beef, tofu, and vegetables, cooking until tender.
3. Dip cooked ingredients into raw egg before eating.

Shabu-Shabu (Japanese Fondue with Wagyu)

Ingredients:

- ½ lb thinly sliced Wagyu beef
- 4 cups dashi broth
- 1 cup Napa cabbage (chopped)
- ½ cup mushrooms
- ½ block tofu (cubed)
- 1 cup udon noodles

Instructions:

1. Heat dashi broth to a simmer.
2. Swish thin slices of meat in the broth until cooked.
3. Add vegetables and tofu, cooking until tender.
4. Serve with ponzu or sesame dipping sauce.

Yakiniku (Japanese BBQ)

Ingredients:

- ½ lb Wagyu beef (thinly sliced)
- 1 tbsp soy sauce
- 1 tbsp sake
- 1 tsp sugar
- ½ tsp sesame oil

Instructions:

1. Mix soy sauce, sake, sugar, and sesame oil.
2. Marinate beef for 15 minutes.
3. Grill over high heat for 1-2 minutes per side.

Unagi Kabayaki (Grilled Eel with Sweet Soy Glaze)

Ingredients:

- 1 eel fillet
- 2 tbsp soy sauce
- 1 tbsp mirin
- 1 tbsp sugar
- 1 tsp sake

Instructions:

1. Grill eel fillet skin-side down until lightly charred.
2. Brush with sauce and grill for another 2-3 minutes.
3. Serve over rice.

Kaiseki Ryori (Traditional Multi-Course Meal)

Sample Courses:

1. **Appetizer:** Seasonal pickles and a small bite of tofu.
2. **Soup:** Matsutake Dobin Mushi (see below).
3. **Sashimi:** Otoro Sashimi (see below).
4. **Grilled Dish:** Yakiniku Wagyu beef.
5. **Steamed Dish:** Chawanmushi (savory egg custard).
6. **Rice Course:** Chirashi Sushi with Premium Seafood.
7. **Dessert:** Matcha ice cream or Anmitsu.

Fugu Sashimi (Blowfish Sashimi)

Ingredients:

- Thinly sliced fugu (blowfish) sashimi
- Ponzu sauce
- Grated daikon and green onions

Instructions:

1. Arrange thinly sliced fugu on a plate in a floral pattern.
2. Serve with ponzu sauce, grated daikon, and green onions.

Matsutake Dobin Mushi (Matsutake Mushroom Soup)

Ingredients:

- 2 cups dashi broth
- ½ cup sliced Matsutake mushrooms
- 2 shrimp (optional)
- 1 slice of yuzu (optional)

Instructions:

1. Heat dashi broth in a small teapot or pot.
2. Add mushrooms and shrimp, simmering for a few minutes.
3. Pour into a small cup and serve with yuzu for aroma.

Kani Nabe (Crab Hot Pot)

Ingredients:

- ½ lb crab legs
- 4 cups dashi broth
- 1 cup Napa cabbage
- ½ cup mushrooms
- ½ block tofu (cubed)

Instructions:

1. Heat dashi broth in a pot.
2. Add crab, tofu, and vegetables.
3. Simmer until crab is cooked through.

Otoro Sashimi (Fatty Tuna Sashimi)

Ingredients:

- ½ lb Otoro (fatty tuna)
- Soy sauce
- Wasabi
- Pickled ginger

Instructions:

1. Slice Otoro into thin pieces.
2. Serve with soy sauce, wasabi, and pickled ginger.

Chirashi Sushi with Premium Seafood

Ingredients:

- 1 cup sushi rice
- ½ lb assorted sashimi (Otoro, Uni, Ikura, etc.)
- 1 tbsp rice vinegar
- ½ tsp sugar
- 1 tsp soy sauce

Instructions:

1. Mix rice vinegar and sugar into warm rice.
2. Arrange premium seafood on top.
3. Drizzle with soy sauce and serve.

Uni Don (Sea Urchin Rice Bowl)

Ingredients:

- 1 cup sushi rice
- ½ cup fresh uni (sea urchin)
- 1 tsp soy sauce
- 1 tsp wasabi
- 1 tbsp ikura (optional)
- Shiso leaf (for garnish)

Instructions:

1. Prepare sushi rice and let it cool slightly.
2. Arrange uni on top of the rice.
3. Drizzle with soy sauce and add a small dab of wasabi.
4. Garnish with ikura and shiso leaf.

Ikura Don (Salmon Roe Rice Bowl)

Ingredients:

- 1 cup sushi rice
- ½ cup ikura (salmon roe)
- 1 tsp soy sauce
- ½ sheet nori (cut into strips)

Instructions:

1. Prepare sushi rice and let it cool slightly.
2. Top with ikura and drizzle with soy sauce.
3. Garnish with nori strips.

Kaisen Don (Mixed Sashimi Rice Bowl)

Ingredients:

- 1 cup sushi rice
- ½ lb assorted sashimi (salmon, tuna, yellowtail, etc.)
- 1 tbsp soy sauce
- ½ tsp wasabi
- ½ sheet nori (cut into strips)

Instructions:

1. Prepare sushi rice and let it cool slightly.
2. Arrange sashimi slices on top.
3. Drizzle with soy sauce and add wasabi.
4. Garnish with nori strips.

Hida Beef Teppanyaki

Ingredients:

- ½ lb Hida beef (thinly sliced)
- 1 tbsp soy sauce
- 1 tbsp mirin
- 1 tsp sesame oil
- ½ cup sliced mushrooms
- ½ cup sliced bell peppers

Instructions:

1. Heat a teppan or griddle over medium-high heat.
2. Cook the beef for 1-2 minutes per side.
3. Add vegetables and stir-fry until tender.
4. Drizzle with soy sauce and mirin before serving.

Kamameshi (Iron Pot Rice with Seafood or Meat)

Ingredients:

- 1 cup short-grain rice
- 2 cups dashi broth
- ½ cup mixed seafood (shrimp, scallops, clams) or chicken
- ½ cup sliced mushrooms
- 1 tbsp soy sauce
- 1 tbsp mirin

Instructions:

1. Rinse rice and place it in an iron pot.
2. Add dashi broth, seafood or meat, and seasonings.
3. Cover and cook on low heat until rice is tender.

Black Cod Saikyo Yaki (Miso-Marinated Black Cod)

Ingredients:

- 2 black cod fillets
- 3 tbsp white miso
- 1 tbsp sake
- 1 tbsp mirin
- 1 tsp sugar

Instructions:

1. Mix miso, sake, mirin, and sugar.
2. Marinate cod fillets for 24 hours.
3. Grill or broil for 5-7 minutes until golden brown.

Nodoguro Shioyaki (Grilled Blackthroat Seaperch)

Ingredients:

- 1 whole nodoguro (blackthroat seaperch)
- 1 tsp salt
- Lemon wedges

Instructions:

1. Sprinkle fish with salt and let rest for 15 minutes.
2. Grill over medium heat until crispy and golden.
3. Serve with lemon wedges.

Anago Meshi (Grilled Sea Eel Over Rice)

Ingredients:

- 1 cup rice
- 1 grilled anago (sea eel) fillet
- 2 tbsp eel sauce (tare)
- ½ sheet nori (cut into strips)

Instructions:

1. Prepare rice and place in a bowl.
2. Top with grilled anago and drizzle with tare sauce.
3. Garnish with nori strips.

Amaebi Sashimi (Sweet Shrimp Sashimi)

Ingredients:

- 6 fresh amaebi (sweet shrimp)
- 1 tsp soy sauce
- ½ tsp wasabi
- 1 shiso leaf

Instructions:

1. Peel and devein amaebi, leaving the tails intact.
2. Serve raw with soy sauce, wasabi, and shiso leaf.

Ise Ebi (Spiny Lobster Sashimi or Grilled)

Ingredients:

- 1 fresh ise ebi (spiny lobster)
- 1 tsp soy sauce
- 1 tsp yuzu juice

Instructions (Sashimi):

1. Remove lobster meat from shell and slice thinly.
2. Serve with soy sauce and yuzu juice.

Instructions (Grilled):

1. Cut lobster in half and brush with soy sauce.
2. Grill shell-side down until meat is opaque.

Kurobuta Tonkatsu (Premium Black Pork Cutlet)

Ingredients:

- 1 kurobuta pork cutlet
- ½ cup panko breadcrumbs
- 1 egg (beaten)
- ½ cup flour
- Oil for frying
- Tonkatsu sauce

Instructions:

1. Dredge pork in flour, dip in egg, then coat with panko.
2. Deep-fry until golden brown and crispy.
3. Serve with tonkatsu sauce.

Soba with Duck Breast

Ingredients:

- 4 oz duck breast
- 1 cup cooked soba noodles
- 2 cups dashi broth
- 1 tbsp soy sauce
- 1 tbsp mirin
- 1 green onion (sliced)

Instructions:

1. Sear duck breast until skin is crispy. Slice thinly.
2. Heat dashi broth, soy sauce, and mirin.
3. Add soba noodles and top with sliced duck.
4. Garnish with green onions.

Dobin Mushi (Tea Pot Steamed Soup)

Ingredients:

- 2 cups dashi broth
- ½ cup sliced Matsutake mushrooms
- 2 shrimp (or chicken pieces)
- 1 small piece yuzu (optional)
- 1 shiso leaf (optional)

Instructions:

1. Heat dashi broth in a small teapot or pot.
2. Add mushrooms and shrimp, simmering gently for a few minutes.
3. Pour the broth into a small cup and serve with a side of yuzu for added aroma.

Miso-Marinated Wagyu

Ingredients:

- ½ lb Wagyu beef steak
- 3 tbsp white miso
- 1 tbsp sake
- 1 tbsp mirin
- 1 tsp sugar

Instructions:

1. Mix miso, sake, mirin, and sugar into a smooth paste.
2. Coat Wagyu steak with the miso marinade and refrigerate for 12-24 hours.
3. Grill or pan-sear over medium-high heat for 2-3 minutes per side.
4. Let rest before slicing and serving.

Nabe with Kobe Beef

Ingredients:

- ½ lb thinly sliced Kobe beef
- 4 cups dashi broth
- 1 cup Napa cabbage (chopped)
- ½ cup mushrooms
- ½ block tofu (cubed)
- 1 carrot (thinly sliced)
- 1 tbsp soy sauce
- 1 tbsp mirin

Instructions:

1. Heat dashi broth in a nabe pot.
2. Add vegetables and tofu, simmering until tender.
3. Swish Kobe beef slices in the broth for a few seconds until cooked.
4. Serve hot with dipping sauces (ponzu or sesame sauce).

Abalone Steak with Butter Sauce

Ingredients:

- 2 fresh abalone (cleaned and shell removed)
- 1 tbsp butter
- 1 tbsp soy sauce
- 1 tsp sake
- 1 garlic clove (minced)

Instructions:

1. Heat butter in a pan over medium heat.
2. Sear abalone for 2-3 minutes per side.
3. Add soy sauce, sake, and garlic, basting the abalone.
4. Slice and serve hot.

Hokkaido Scallop Sashimi

Ingredients:

- 4 fresh Hokkaido scallops
- 1 tsp soy sauce
- ½ tsp wasabi
- 1 shiso leaf

Instructions:

1. Slice scallops into thin pieces.
2. Arrange on a plate with a shiso leaf.
3. Serve with soy sauce and wasabi.

Ankimo (Monkfish Liver)

Ingredients:

- 1 monkfish liver (cleaned)
- 1 tbsp sake
- 1 tbsp mirin
- 1 tbsp soy sauce
- ½ tsp salt
- 1 tbsp grated daikon

Instructions:

1. Soak monkfish liver in saltwater for 30 minutes.
2. Rinse, then marinate in sake for 10 minutes.
3. Roll into a cylinder using plastic wrap and steam for 15-20 minutes.
4. Slice and serve with soy sauce and grated daikon.

Crab Miso Soup with Fresh Snow Crab

Ingredients:

- 4 cups dashi broth
- ½ cup crab meat (snow crab)
- 2 tbsp miso paste
- 1 green onion (chopped)

Instructions:

1. Heat dashi broth in a pot.
2. Dissolve miso paste into the broth.
3. Add crab meat and simmer for 5 minutes.
4. Garnish with green onions and serve hot.

Yakitori Omakase (Grilled Skewers with Premium Ingredients)

Ingredients:

- 2 chicken thighs (cut into bite-sized pieces)
- 2 chicken livers (optional)
- 2 Kobe beef cubes
- 2 king prawns
- 2 shiitake mushrooms
- 1 tbsp soy sauce
- 1 tbsp sake
- 1 tbsp mirin

Instructions:

1. Skewer each ingredient separately.
2. Grill over high heat, brushing with a soy sauce-mirin glaze.
3. Cook each skewer until charred and tender.

Toro Taku Roll (Fatty Tuna & Pickled Radish Roll)

Ingredients:

- 1 cup sushi rice
- ½ sheet nori
- ¼ cup chopped fatty tuna (toro)
- 2 tbsp pickled daikon (takuan)

Instructions:

1. Lay nori on a bamboo sushi mat.
2. Spread rice evenly, leaving a small border.
3. Add chopped toro and takuan.
4. Roll tightly, slice, and serve.

Sazae Tsuboyaki (Grilled Turban Shell)

Ingredients:

- 2 sazae (turban shells)
- 1 tbsp soy sauce
- 1 tbsp sake
- ½ tsp mirin

Instructions:

1. Place turban shells directly on a grill over medium heat.
2. Pour soy sauce, sake, and mirin inside the shell as it cooks.
3. Grill until the liquid is bubbling and the meat is tender.

Ishikari Nabe (Salmon Hot Pot)

Ingredients:

- 2 salmon fillets (cut into chunks)
- 4 cups dashi broth
- 1 cup Napa cabbage (chopped)
- ½ cup daikon (sliced)
- ½ cup carrots (sliced)
- ½ block tofu (cubed)
- 2 tbsp miso paste
- 1 tbsp sake
- 1 green onion (chopped)

Instructions:

1. Heat dashi broth in a nabe pot.
2. Dissolve miso paste and add sake.
3. Add vegetables and tofu, simmering until tender.
4. Add salmon and cook for 3-4 minutes until just done.
5. Garnish with green onions and serve hot.

Karei Karaage (Deep-Fried Flounder)

Ingredients:

- 1 whole flounder (cleaned and cut into pieces)
- ½ cup potato starch (or cornstarch)
- 1 tsp salt
- Oil for deep-frying
- Lemon wedges

Instructions:

1. Pat dry the flounder pieces and season with salt.
2. Coat lightly with potato starch.
3. Deep-fry at 350°F (175°C) until golden and crispy.
4. Drain excess oil and serve with lemon wedges.

Botan Ebi Sashimi (Large Sweet Shrimp)

Ingredients:

- 4 fresh botan ebi (large sweet shrimp)
- 1 tsp soy sauce
- ½ tsp wasabi
- Shiso leaf for garnish

Instructions:

1. Peel and devein the shrimp, keeping the tails intact.
2. Serve raw with soy sauce and wasabi on the side.
3. Garnish with a shiso leaf.

Shojin Ryori (Buddhist Vegan Cuisine)

Ingredients:

- ½ block tofu (grilled or steamed)
- ½ cup simmered root vegetables (daikon, carrots, lotus root)
- ¼ cup blanched spinach (seasoned with sesame)
- ½ cup miso soup
- 1 bowl steamed rice

Instructions:

1. Prepare each component separately using dashi made from kombu (seaweed).
2. Serve the dishes in small portions, arranged harmoniously.

Tosa Zukuri (Seared Bonito Sashimi)

Ingredients:

- ½ lb bonito fillet
- 1 tbsp soy sauce
- ½ tbsp yuzu juice
- 1 green onion (sliced)
- 1-inch piece ginger (grated)

Instructions:

1. Sear the outside of the bonito fillet using a kitchen torch or grill.
2. Slice into thin pieces and arrange on a plate.
3. Garnish with green onions and grated ginger.
4. Serve with soy sauce and yuzu juice.

Tai Chazuke (Sea Bream Over Rice with Tea)

Ingredients:

- 1 cup steamed rice
- ½ cup fresh sea bream sashimi
- ½ cup hot dashi or green tea
- ½ sheet nori (cut into strips)
- 1 tsp sesame seeds
- 1 tsp soy sauce

Instructions:

1. Place rice in a bowl and top with sea bream sashimi.
2. Pour hot dashi or tea over the fish.
3. Garnish with nori strips and sesame seeds.
4. Drizzle with soy sauce before serving.

Kinmedai Nitsuke (Simmered Golden Eye Snapper)

Ingredients:

- 1 fillet kinmedai (golden eye snapper)
- ½ cup dashi broth
- 2 tbsp soy sauce
- 1 tbsp sake
- 1 tbsp mirin
- 1 tsp sugar
- 1-inch piece ginger (sliced)

Instructions:

1. Heat dashi broth, soy sauce, sake, mirin, and sugar in a pan.
2. Add kinmedai fillet and simmer for 10 minutes.
3. Baste the fish with the sauce while cooking.
4. Serve with the reduced sauce and garnish with ginger slices.

Hamo Ryori (Pike Conger Eel Dishes)

Ingredients:

- 1 fillet hamo (pike conger eel)
- 2 cups dashi broth
- 1 tbsp soy sauce
- 1 tbsp mirin
- 1 tsp grated yuzu zest

Instructions:

1. Score the hamo fillet finely to remove small bones.
2. Poach in hot dashi broth for 1-2 minutes.
3. Serve with soy sauce, mirin, and a touch of yuzu zest.

Tataki Style Wagyu Beef

Ingredients:

- ½ lb Wagyu beef (sirloin or tenderloin)
- 1 tbsp soy sauce
- 1 tbsp ponzu sauce
- ½ tsp grated garlic
- ½ tsp grated ginger
- 1 green onion (sliced)

Instructions:

1. Sear the outside of the Wagyu beef on high heat for about 30 seconds per side.
2. Slice thinly and arrange on a plate.
3. Garnish with green onions, garlic, and ginger.
4. Serve with ponzu sauce.

Kinki Nitsuke (Simmered Channel Rockfish)

Ingredients:

- 1 whole kinki fish (cleaned)
- ½ cup dashi broth
- 2 tbsp soy sauce
- 1 tbsp mirin
- 1 tbsp sake
- 1 tsp sugar
- 1-inch piece ginger (sliced)

Instructions:

1. Heat dashi broth, soy sauce, mirin, sake, and sugar in a pan.
2. Add kinki fish and simmer for 10-15 minutes, basting occasionally.
3. Serve with reduced sauce and garnish with ginger slices.

Premium Hokkaido Uni Pasta

Ingredients:

- ½ cup fresh Hokkaido uni (sea urchin)
- 6 oz pasta (spaghetti or linguine)
- 2 tbsp butter
- 1 tbsp heavy cream
- 1 tbsp soy sauce
- ½ tsp lemon juice
- ½ tsp black pepper

Instructions:

1. Cook pasta according to package instructions.
2. Melt butter in a pan, then add heavy cream and soy sauce.
3. Add half of the uni and gently mash it into the sauce.
4. Toss in the cooked pasta and mix well.
5. Plate and top with remaining uni, a drizzle of lemon juice, and black pepper.

Miso Black Cod with Truffle Oil

Ingredients:

- 2 black cod fillets
- 3 tbsp white miso paste
- 2 tbsp mirin
- 1 tbsp sake
- 1 tbsp sugar
- ½ tsp truffle oil
- 1 tbsp neutral oil (for searing)

Instructions:

1. Mix miso paste, mirin, sake, and sugar into a marinade.
2. Coat the cod fillets and marinate for at least 24 hours.
3. Preheat oven to 400°F (200°C).
4. Wipe off excess marinade and sear cod in a pan with neutral oil.
5. Transfer to oven and bake for 10 minutes.
6. Drizzle with truffle oil before serving.

Foie Gras Chawanmushi (Steamed Egg Custard with Foie Gras)

Ingredients:

- 2 eggs
- 1 ¼ cups dashi broth
- 1 tbsp soy sauce
- 1 tsp mirin
- 2 small foie gras slices
- ½ tsp black truffle shavings (optional)

Instructions:

1. Whisk eggs gently, mix with dashi, soy sauce, and mirin.
2. Strain the mixture and pour into small cups.
3. Add a foie gras slice to each cup.
4. Steam for 12-15 minutes over low heat.
5. Garnish with black truffle shavings.

Grilled King Crab Legs

Ingredients:

- 2 large king crab legs
- 2 tbsp melted butter
- ½ tsp sea salt
- ½ tsp lemon juice

Instructions:

1. Preheat grill to medium-high heat.
2. Brush crab legs with melted butter and sprinkle with sea salt.
3. Grill for 4-5 minutes per side until heated through.
4. Finish with lemon juice before serving.

White Truffle Soba

Ingredients:

- 6 oz soba noodles
- 1 tbsp soy sauce
- 1 tbsp dashi broth
- ½ tsp truffle oil
- ½ tsp white truffle shavings

Instructions:

1. Cook soba noodles according to package instructions, then rinse in cold water.
2. Toss with soy sauce, dashi broth, and truffle oil.
3. Plate and garnish with white truffle shavings.

A5 Wagyu Sukiyaki with Truffle Egg Dip

Ingredients:

- ½ lb A5 Wagyu beef (thinly sliced)
- 2 cups sukiyaki broth (soy sauce, mirin, sake, sugar)
- ½ cup Napa cabbage (chopped)
- ½ block tofu (cubed)
- ½ cup shiitake mushrooms
- 1 egg yolk
- ½ tsp truffle oil

Instructions:

1. Heat sukiyaki broth in a shallow pan.
2. Add vegetables and tofu, cooking until tender.
3. Quickly sear Wagyu slices in the broth.
4. Mix egg yolk with truffle oil and use as a dip for Wagyu.

Lobster Miso Ramen

Ingredients:

- 1 lobster (split in half)
- 4 cups dashi broth
- 2 tbsp miso paste
- 2 tbsp mirin
- 2 packs fresh ramen noodles
- ½ cup shiitake mushrooms (sliced)
- 1 green onion (chopped)

Instructions:

1. Boil dashi broth and whisk in miso paste and mirin.
2. Add lobster and simmer for 5 minutes.
3. Cook ramen noodles separately and divide into bowls.
4. Pour broth over noodles and top with lobster, mushrooms, and green onions.

www.ingramcontent.com/pod-product-compliance
Lightning Source LLC
LaVergne TN
LVHW081500060526
838201LV00056BA/2857